A TALE IN TH1

# GOBLINS

# JEN CALLEJA & RACHEL LOUISE HODGSON

ROUGH TRADE BOOKS × MUSEUM OF WITCHCRAFT AND MAGIC

# DEFINE GOBLIN

For me, anything that behaves mischievously and in its own best interest, that is bold and all body, could be a goblin, though this does not necessarily mean they are evil or cruel. Above all, a goblin is shameless. A goblin has no shame. This is my personal history of goblinry.

# PART ONE

# GOBLINHOOD

## GOBLIN MATINEE

A lot of people are scared of puppets. There's something about their uncanniness that disturbs us. But I feel like I was brought up by them. I learned the alphabet from *Sesame Street* (I still say 'zee' and 'haitch'). I thought the Psammead—the small, hairy, grumpy sand-fairy from the nineties programme *Five Children and It* (1991)—looked exactly like my grandad when he had his shirt off. All my favourite TV programmes and films as a kid born in '86 had them in: soft, furry, fleshy, wet-looking, dead-eyed, blinking, toothy, gummy creatures that moved of their own volition. Even when I could see the strings or the wires, or surmised a hand out of shot, or couldn't see them breathe, they still felt very real to me, these mischievous creatures that always had the potential to be either malicious or benign.

There was some contention around what was appropriate viewing for children back in the 80s, and much of what my parents let me watch was actually terrifying and arguably traumatised me and thousands of other kids. Whether or not this is actually the case, I feel like the stories and messages and morals that these films and programmes gave me, as I watched them over and over again until the video warped, became the foundation of my existence in part due to their puppet eeriness.

At the Kino Museum-Lichtspiele in Munich they have shown *The Rocky Horror Picture Show* (1975) every Friday and Saturday night since 1977. My fantasy forever-screening in a cinema would be the things I watched that have left the biggest impression on me, the big cult puppet fantasies: *Labyrinth* (1986) every Friday and as part of a Saturday matinee double bill with *Return to Oz* (1985). *The Dark Crystal* (1982) would show one Sunday a month, and before every screening there would be one of the fourteen episodes of *The Storyteller* (1987) instead of trailers. There'd also be books for sale where you get your popcorn and pick 'n' mix: Angela Carter's *The Bloody Chamber* (1979) and a dozen other books I would have specially selected.

I've been re-watching the above almost constantly over the last couple of years. Even now as a thirty-three-year old I find them comforting, and they still give me goose bumps; I still cry and cheer in the same places. But who I identify with, and how I understand their stories, has changed over time. I see characters in a new light, or the morals or endings don't sit with me as well as they used to, or I've become more interested in who's pulling the strings.

# GOBLINHOOD

I was an odd, unsocialised, lone little goblin as a child. I would shut myself away in my room when the sun went down with the lights off and the TV on, my nose inches from the screen, like a creature looking down a well or into a mirror. I was a sinful, roguish little goblin. My mum was mortified when I started humping a cushion in front of my great aunt when I was a toddler, and equally so when I snuck up behind her and pinched her bum in Woolworths, making her let out an involuntary shriek when I was about four. She used to take me swimming on Sundays when I was five or six and I once refused to leave the pool, pointing at her and shouting 'Stranger! Stranger!' to her cringing horror. I was a brown, dark-haired, dark-eyed, hairy little goblin. Children would point at the hair down my legs and my arms and on my face and call me monkey or, even worse, a boy. I wasn't like the well-groomed, mostly blonde and mousey children at school. I was feral-looking. And I was a girl, therefore a particularly furtive, gooey, twitchy, alarming little goblin.

I often related much more with the beasts in *The Storyteller*— the Jim Henson-produced, Anthony Minghella-scribed children's series—than I did with the heroes and heroines. These fourteen adaptations of fables and fairytales are filled with horrible *things*. There are fuming, goblinish devils and the dome-headed goblinesque Death in 'The Soldier and Death'; the pot-bellied demon whose legs walk around torsoless in 'Fearnot'; the awful trolls with rings through their noses who keep a young Jane Horrocks as a servant in 'The True Bride'; Medusa in 'Perseus and the Gorgon' has animatronic snakes for hair; the storyteller himself—played by John Hurt—is now rumoured to have been a goblin all along.

I felt more connected to the Straggletag than her beautiful alter-ego, the title character in the episode 'Sapsorrow'; a version of Cinderella with a young French and Saunders playing her morally ugly sisters. Sapsorrow is hidden under fur and feathers after running away from another kingdom because the law decrees she would have to marry the King, her own father (you can't get more patriarchal than that) because her dead mother's ring fits her wedding finger. She becomes the Straggletag, a servant in a prince's castle in a land far away, and everyone finds the Straggletag repulsive. The Prince must marry the Straggletag when the shoe Sapsorrow leaves behind at the third ball he throws in her honour fits 'her'.

As the Straggletag she has a looser gait; a cool, lumbering, freeing genderlessness in her dungarees. (Incidentally, you can tell *The Storyteller* had a music video maker as its cinematographer from its dramatic, dingy, woozy look: the various castle chambers, with light slanting through twilit windows and candlelit chandeliers, give you the impression that the androgynous musician Prince—who almost played the Goblin King in *Labyrinth*—might strut in at any minute). She is often referred to as dirty, filthy, though there is only dirt under her nails from working. Her coat actually looks soft, and carries mice in it! She has the same piercing eyes and throaty Irish accent as Sapsorrow. As Straggletag she teases the Prince, who longs for Sapsorrow. He seems at ease with Straggletag, even if her sarcasm and frankness go a little far sometimes for his liking, "no one else in the whole palace, in the whole kingdom, talks to me like you do". Sapsorrow is timid, frozen, perfection, flighty, delicate, silent. The Prince's reward for agreeing to marry Straggletag and breaking her cursed life is he gets beautiful, carefree, fair-skinned, hairless Sapsorrow, unsullied by past trauma and a sharp tongue. Straggletag/Sapsorrow's reward? Marrying a charmless prince who even pushes her over with the sole of his boot while she scrubs the floor for giving him lip. She escapes one befitting role for another.

The brother episode to 'Sapsorrow' is 'Hans My Hedgehog', about a hedgehog boy born "ugly as sin, sprouting hair everywhere" to a couple who can't have children. The mother prays to have any kind of child, "a thing made of marzipan or porridge", and has a hedgehog baby, who the villagers ridicule with the name Grovelhog and who the father finds beastly. Hans eventually leaves his family and the village, and his father only realises how soft his quills are when he hugs him goodbye. (This makes me cry every time.) When Hans is to marry a Princess, the Princess wants to break the curse of his hedgehogness. He tells her not to tell a soul that he takes off his quills when the sun goes down for three nights in order to break the spell. Her mother guesses that he's bewitched and tells her to throw his quills on the fire when he strips them off that night. She throws them on the fire and he runs off, only to be found years later by the Princess, who breaks the curse with true love, which... turns him into a boring, unbeastly, classically handsome man, like at the end of *Beauty and the Beast*. (Such disappointment when the morose but charming Beast turns into a sprightly, uber-positive blonde.)

How would I find love if I was always going to be a Grovelhog, the Straggletag? Would I, too, have to transform? I remember asking my Anglo-Irish mum (moon-skinned and black-haired like Snow White, green-eyed like the Evil Queen) how she knew my dad, a Maltese immigrant recently arrived from the Mediterranean at the time they met, was 'the one'. She told me that it was when they were in the back of a taxi and he ran his fingers over the hair on her top lip and then kissed her. The hair, after all, was soft. I'm basking in my back garden like a toad on a rock right now and the hair on my legs and under my armpits and on my lip is long and dark and shiny and silky. I like the way the hair on my arms and legs pokes through my tattoos, like weeds growing in the ruins of long-vacated castles.

## GOBLIN MOTHERHOOD

—

"You must defend your dreams, you can't let the world take away your dreams from you, that's your most prized possession."
—Walter Murch, director of *Return to Oz*.

—

"There's a moment in old age when some people become a little girl again"
—Eva Wiseman on Paula Rego, *The Guardian* 2018

*Return to Oz* is the terrifying non-musical sequel to one of the most famous musicals of all time. Dorothy Gale escapes a sanitorium (yep, this is a children's film) where she is meant to be treated for delusions and insomnia caused by her first escapade in Oz. She ends up back there where she has to fight Wheelers (like '77 punks with squeaky wheels instead of feet) and Princess Mombi (who can take her head off and replace it with the stolen heads of women she keeps in a room of glass display cases [yep, still a children's film]) to get to the Nome King flanked by gargoyles up in his mountain to demand he returns the Emerald City to its former splendour.

The film's director Walter Murch was shocked and hurt that people found the film so petrifying, and the backlash basically ruined his career as a film director. In one interview he says that he believes one reason people found it so frightening is that it's not a musical—there aren't any jolly songs to break the terror. A second reason is because Dorothy is actually played by a young girl—an eleven-year-old Fairuza Balk, who would go on to star in *The Craft* (1996). Another reason he thinks the film scared people is that Auntie Em, the mother figure in the film, doesn't get mother's intuition and take Dorothy home immediately from the creepy sanitorium where she had taken her for 'electric healing' for her insomnia ("you're no help to me in the morning") and hallucinations. Why doesn't Auntie Em twig that something super sinister is going on? Doesn't she care? Nothing's scarier than a bad mother.

There's a profile-interview with the Portuguese-born, London-based artist Paula Rego that I think about often. The piece covers how she has always been afraid in her life, about how she did a series of drawings about her depression where she's holding things "that do not help" (like Sarah holding onto her toys and magazines in her replica room in the junkyard in *Labyrinth*) and how Rego's children always felt like the 'subplot' in the story of her art, and in her dreamworld. The interviewer comments on how frail Rego has become: "Interviewing somebody who has become very old very quickly feels both important—gather what you can before it's too late—and exploitative, and afterwards I take the long way back to work to shake off my discomfort". The interviewer seems uncomfortable about Rego's vulnerability— Rego has transformed into something else, something other, both because of her age and her mental illness.

For a long time I used to think of my own mother as a kind of goblin because of her manic depression and her distance. She has always been in her own world. She was first sectioned for her mental health long before I was born, and was in and out of hospital for long and short stints during my childhood. She wasn't a mother one could confide in, and she didn't notice when something was wrong. I often felt invisible. When I hurtled down into my teens, I began feeling like she was selfish. I was angry that she was so self-centred. There was also something about how unpredictable and unkempt and sedate and eventually immobile she became through illness, something of the *grotesque* about her that unnerved me.

When I got older, I began to understand that my mum wasn't Auntie Em, an unperceptive and unthinking mother, she was more like Dorothy. Like Dorothy, she was overwhelmed by preoccupations. Like Dorothy, she was probably considered a nuisance because she couldn't work from being so tired and sick. Like Dorothy, she was a little girl, having been held in a kind of stasis because of her illness. Unlike Dorothy, she did have to endure electric shock therapy. She must have been terrified and have felt so alone. I realise that I probably projected my shame and fear onto her, and made her into a monster. Now, I empathise with her, and understand the feeling of wanting to remain in a world of your own making as a way of coping in a hard and complicated reality.

## GOBLIN LOGIC
—

"The usual is the structural in a temporal form"
—Sara Ahmed
—

"If you call out a goblin, you become a goblin."
—Sara Ahmed (impishly paraphrased)
—

*Labyrinth*, the deranged, coming-of-age, cult classic goblin musical, stars David Bowie as Jareth the Goblin King and a fourteen-year-old Jennifer Connolly as Sarah. After wishing the Goblin King would take away her baby half-brother, Sarah has to traverse a maze to get to the castle high up in the centre of the labyrinth to get him back from Jareth without being captured, distracted from her quest, falling into the Bog of Eternal Stench, or seduced by the Goblin King. *Labyrinth* is an anti-fairytale, there's no marrying the Goblin King, who is revealed to be nothing more than the fantasy of patriarchal control of Sarah's making. "Fear me, love me, do as I say and I will be your slave," Jareth almost begs Sarah.

One of Sarah's most crucial lines in the film, and one often quoted as empowering in listicles (there are many: You Have No Power Over Me: Life Lessons from *Labyrinth*; 14 lessons We Learned from *Labyrinth*; What I learned from *Labyrinth*) is:

*It's not fair... But that's the way it is!*

This is Sarah's moment of epiphany when she realises that getting frustrated and declaring things constantly unfair is pointless (as Jareth/Bowie says to her at one point: "I wonder what your basis for comparison is"). It used to be a go-to motto for me, a way to let things go and absolve myself from responsibility. Until, that is, I realised how defeatist and awkwardly passive it is. Maybe you could see it as realising the world is skewed for some people so you're not being personally victimised, but ultimately, it's like saying 'it's shit, but what can you do, what's the point in complaining.'

Much of the time when Sarah says that things aren't fair, they actually aren't! She has been set an impossible task, The Fireys try to take off her head, Jareth spikes her peach, the rules change constantly. She's in a labyrinthine system where she's tricked and tripped up. She has every right to complain. When I hear that phrase now, I think of Susan Fowler, who exposed the sexist discrimination she experienced while working at Uber: "And I reported it to HR and they said, 'Yes, you know, he shouldn't have done this. But unfortunately, that's the way it is'." And Daphne Caruana Galizia, the murdered Maltese journalist who exposed the Maltese elites' involvement in the Panama Papers scandal: "It's true that life is unfair and that much of it can't be helped, but where I can do anything to avoid unfairness or to set it straight, then I will."

I think Sarah's false epiphany set me back a matter of years.

## THE STORYTELLER,
## THE PUPPETEER & THE VENTRILOQUIST

Take a lantern, it's dark in the woods, but not for long. There's a clearing ahead, you can see the glow in the distance. What you see in front of you aren't apparitions but fourteen television screens, a few partially submerged in the forest floor, or in a pile of leaves, or sunken into the trunk of a tree. On each screen is a looped episode of *The Storyteller*. There's 'Fearnot' (based on the story 'The Boy Who Went Forth to Learn How to Shudder'), 'The Three Ravens', 'The Luck Child', 'The Heartless Giant', 'Theseus and the Minotaur' (set, of course, in a labyrinth) and more. I've got them synced to all start playing the theme music simultaneously: A stabbing cello joined by a breathy flute with a crow cawing over it—it still gives me the heebie-jeebies. John Hurt, who plays the storyteller himself, speaks over the music in an echoey voice, listen!

*When people told themselves their past with stories, explained their present with stories, foretold their future with stories, the best place by the fire was kept for: The Storyteller.*

While the final dregs of a clarinet toot off, some words appear over a fire that say something like 'From a traditional German folktale' or a Russian fable, before Hurt's face appears, knobbly with cheek and nose prosthetics, and he begins his distinctive way of weaving these old yarns, full of 'dearies' (referring to the viewers, or his talking dog) and his ominous, low-registered 'oh dearrr, oh dearrr' to warn of impending doom.

Stories used to roam free and ride in storytellers' minds, worn smooth like a well-sucked lozenge in a storyteller's mouth. Sometimes they tweak the recipe for the story soup. Rebecca Solnit read fairytales online for her nieces and nephews and the rest of the world during the coronavirus lockdown and made little alterations—the Little Mermaid returns to her sisters, for instance, and she's previously retold Cinderella where everyone, including the evil sisters and the stepmother, are freed from their roles. But now, my dearies, stories are usually set in stone. We no longer need storytellers to pass on stories, they're transported by print. The old stories multiplied and became furnished with new details, and we can no longer see the connection with the old stories.

It was the way John Hurt told the stories that made them for me, the rhythm of his voice, his presence that ran like a thread through all the stories. More and more often, famous writers are asked to adapt old stories, Rebecca Solnit, or Neil Gaiman, for instance, who retold Norse fairytales, who's currently remaking *The Storyteller* series in fact. I wish translators of literature were viewed as storytellers. People seem wary of the idea, but translators don't even alter the stories they tell, they try their best to keep every detail. I think it's because people think to themselves: 'Who is this nobody telling me a story? Where's Neil Gaiman?' (I think I just saw him wandering in the bushes, going through some kind of transformation...)

In the making-of documentary for the new Netflix remake of another of my childhood favourites, Jim Henson's *The Dark Crystal,* one of the puppeteers says something that could be about being a literary translator:

*I don't think puppeteers are well known, by the nature of their job they are hidden. There are very few famous puppeteers, it is an art where you choose to hide. And I very much think it's like a musician, that you have an instrument and you play a beautiful tune on it and it's the tune we remember, it's not necessarily the piano it was played on.*

And yet an instrument is as inert as a wooden puppet without someone to play it, and there are those that will play it well or play it less well. Translators are like ventriloquists, but we're also the ventriloquist's dummy. We do the voices, but our every move is guided by the texts we translate. Can you tell it's our voice every time? A voice I find comforting is Brian Henson's. He did the voice for the goblin Hoggle in *Labyrinth*, the dog in *The Storyteller*, Jack Pumpkinhead in *Return to Oz*. His voice is so distinctive, but changes subtly every time. It has its own particular qualities.

Elsewhere in the documentary, actor Simon Pegg could also be talking about translation. He even unknowingly critiques the well-worn metaphor that reading a translation is like looking through a pane of clear glass:

*The point with puppetry is it's a medium, it's an artform in itself and that's what you're watching, it helps you stay slightly detached and think about it a bit more, you don't just get hypnotised by it, looking through a window, you know, you're looking at something which is a representation.*

Translation would be better off recognised as something else entirely, not an unblocked view directly to the original work of literature, but to a performance or retelling of it.

If you go straight ahead you'll come to my workshop where I've been making alterations. Come in and warm up, I have a fire going. You can sit there, by the workbench. I've been inserting translators' photos and opening remarks into copies of their translations on the sly and planting them in bookshops. "From a contemporary German novel" or "From a modern Turkish book of short stories" is now on the title page. The moment you see and hear them introduce the story, you know that everything that comes after is a retelling. Here's a batch I've been working on for Emily Wilson. Here's a photo of her reading her translation of *The Odyssey* (2018) to her three daughters and three cats. I've carefully pasted it into copies of the book alongside a photo of her giving a reading from it in New York with her arms raised and accompanied by shadow puppets on the wall behind her, and a photo of her in a school production of *The Odyssey* as a young girl. It's the first translation into English by a woman, and is unblighted by the *inserted* not *translated* misogyny of some of her male predecessors' attempts. Rebecca Solnit wrote an essay called 'The Storykiller and His Sentence' about Harvey Weinstein and how he, as the "king of the storykillers", had the power to tell stories and make other stories go away. All storytellers have power, be they writers, tellers or translators. I like the way Rebecca Solnit tells the stories of others, the rhythm of her voice, her presence that runs through all her essays. I like the way certain translators tell the stories of others, the rhythm of their voices, their presence that runs through their translations.

I wonder if I will get to see all the stories of my childhood remade, and I wonder who'll do the remaking?

## GOBLIN MARKET

A reading of Christina Rossetti's poem 'Goblin Market' (1862) is as a warning against sexual temptation and a celebration of the bond of sisterly love for young girls through the story of two sisters: one won't take the fruit offered by the goblin merchants, while her sister falls for their offer with almost fatal consequences.

When Jareth gives Sarah a poisoned peach in *Labyrinth*, it makes her fall into a deep trance, and she dreams of dancing with him at a masquerade ball where the guests all wear goblin masks and cackle with lascivious mirth.

## THE GIRL WHO WENT OUT
## TO LEARN WHAT FEAR WAS

Like Fearnot who went out into the world because he had never experienced terror, I left a haunted home at eighteen to learn how to live a little. All the warnings about how goblins don't always look like goblins I'd learned from *Labyrinth* and, in the meantime, how wolves might be furry on the inside from Angela Carter's *The Bloody Chamber*, had vanished from my mind. It's as if you reach teenagehood and you forget everything you've ever learned so you have to experience it for yourself.

The small club The Atomic Café in Munich—which used to be on the Neuturmstrasse in the Old Town before it got turned into a Prada and a WeWork—was an enchanted place for me. I would be there three times a week or more dancing and watching bands I'd be lucky to see in a huge venue back home. It ended up becoming a place where I would encounter three goblin musicians.

The first I'll call The Storyteller. A roadie told me I had been selected from the crowd by The Storyteller, a famous musician, to keep him company because his wife had given birth that day in a distant kingdom and he was feeling lonely. No matter how much of a fan I was of his music, no matter how flattered I was, I refused. I wasn't a *groupie*. I would later see him making out with two even younger girls. (He's now a philanthropist for girls trying to start bands and campaigns for gender equality!)

The second I'll call the Marquis after the character in the title story of *The Bloody Chamber*, a retelling of the story of Bluebeard who kept a collection of murdered wives in a locked chamber. I was taken to the Marquis backstage as an offering from his band's manager, who had picked me out of the queue before the show. I convinced myself nothing would happen. The bewitchment was immediate. He was in love with me, he said, he wanted to marry me and move to Paris, like in a fairytale. He wanted me to have his children, he said, could we have babies? I got away just before the tour bus left. I was besotted. Then I got curious and, *oh dear, oh dear, what's this?*, posted about our secret encounter on a thread deep on the band's online forum, and, *oh no!*, opened wide his bloody chamber. I got messages from girls from every stop on the tour, including a fifteen-year-old he had taken semi-prisoner on the tour bus, who he'd plied with drugs, and who he had abandoned in the middle of nowhere. He discovered my indiscretion and told me I would never hear from him again as punishment.

Then there was the Goblin King. Unlike Sarah in *Labyrinth*, I fell for the lure of being a muse in exchange for the most minor attention. He played in one of the most well-known bands in the city. He was older than me, tall, with shoulder-length blonde hair always over one eye, he chain-smoked, and dressed like he was in the 70s rather than the early 00s. He would show up at my bedsit out of the blue like Jareth, and would be otherwise uncontactable. His assistant would sometimes text me in the early hours of the morning to warn me he was on his way over and very drunk. He would laugh at my sad expression as I watched him wander around the Atomic being adored and pretending I didn't exist, like Jareth slipping between the masquerade revellers. He would take me on silent rides in his car and play songs he had written about me. I would wait for the glimmer of the online motif under his photo on MySpace, like a creature in the bushes outside my prey's house waiting for the lights to come on. I lost my mind. My periods inexplicably stopped, I thought it was from the stress and the loneliness. I wrote a long piece about the pain he was causing me and I watched him read it while we sat drinking milkshakes in a McDonald's. He didn't say anything. I moved back to England in the summer.

## GOBLIN MARKET II

Kinuko Y. Craft, a Japanese-American artist, reframed Christina Rossetti's poem by showing the sisters succumbing to the goblins in a lustful orgy, surrounded by bum peaches and penis fruit in a series of illustrations published in *Playboy* magazine. So what if girls want to frolic with goblins?

## THE GIRL WHO WENT OUT
## TO LEARN HOW TO SHUDDER

"I'm exhausted from living up to your expectations of me."
—Jareth to Sarah, *Labyrinth*

I didn't tell you the whole story about the Storyteller, the Marquis and the Goblin King, *I was being mischievous!* To be honest, it's my story, and I'll tell you what I want to tell you. This essay isn't actually my life, you're not looking in through my window, it's merely a representation, one I choose to share. It's only "based on a true story." I was withholding my goblin nature because I didn't think you would be able to take it, it's probably not what you were expecting. I'm not going to tell you about visits to their hotel rooms in different cities years later, or contorting in the dark for the bloodshot eye of a camera, or the friends I abandoned for the possibility of a rendezvous, or pulling on the strings of these goblins' aging vanity when they weren't up for performing. It's hard to resist a goblin, even the most heinous, especially when you're young and have goblinish desires all your own. You can't tell whether you're bewitching them or they're bewitching you, especially when you were brought up to expect a goblin seduction eventually.

I'll tell you this though: When I returned to Munich the following summer to 'break the spell' like Dorothy does in *Return to Oz* and move on with my life, the dynamics had changed between me and the Goblin King. He had dropped the act of being cruel and aloof, maybe like Jareth he had been playing a role, or maybe I didn't buy it anymore; he had no power over me. I felt like I could tell him that I had been pregnant that previous summer, and that I had lost the baby. He seemed repentant about the way he had treated me, he realised now, he said, that he had liked me a lot, hadn't I noticed that he came to see me in the middle of the night and didn't do that for just anybody? On my last night in the city he came over to see me and told me he had always loved me. I said and felt nothing. The Goblin King had lost his goblin nature. For a while he would send me a sincere email every Christmas. He stopped smoking. He lays flower emojis under my birthday Instagram pictures and posts blurry pictures of smoothies and glasses of wine on social media. He now trades cryptocurrencies for a living. *Shudder.* I have to admit, I'm disappointed that he turned into a human.

# WOLFGANG PUPPET

Doyle Wolfgang von Frankenstein, guitarist with cult horror punk band The Misfits (who refers to himself during his teenage years in the band as a "foetus"), went vegan with the encouragement of his girlfriend Alissa White-Gluz, lead singer of the Swedish metal band Arch Enemy. "I'm so much healthier [now]," he says in an interview in *The Village Voice*, "I feel it's ethical. It isn't just for health reasons; it's for not leaving a big carbon footprint of myself, you know, a trail of fucking death and destruction." My friend Tom made me a cute puppet of Doyle for Christmas last year. I think it fits this mellower, more human Doyle: he may still wear corpse paint, be ripped and play his guitar by punching it, but he now obsessively posts pictures online of cute animals, Alissa his 'Queenbeast', fan art, and his favourite vegan baked goods.

# PART TWO

# ART GOBLINS

## CROTCH GOBLINS

Let me magically populate the room before you with babies.

Sitting up against that pile of straw is the Hans the Hedgehog baby puppet, a clear ancestor of the baby from *Dinosaurs* (1991). (They're related by Jim Henson's Creature Shop).

Wrapped in a sheet on that bed is a white-faced doll. The witch, played by Miranda Richardson, replaces the Princess's baby with it while she's sleeping in the episode of *The Storyteller* called 'The Three Ravens'. (What makes this scene so terrifying is that when Joely Richardson's mute Princess awakens to find her newborn baby is a creepy doll there is absolutely no music, and she gives a silent scream. The silence beside the soundless scream and the baby doll's painted face is blood-curdling.)

In that plain white cot over there is both a hyperreal replica of a baby and a Werepup. (These baby replicas are called 'reborns' by the women who care for them either because they can't have children or don't want them yet or who have adult children who've left home. Werepups are werewolf puppy dolls created by artist Asia Eriksen for people to 'adopt' in order to manage their anxiety or as a tribute to a lost loved one).

In a glass-topped case is the white and red striped romper worn by Toby the baby in *Labyrinth*. (Himself now a puppeteer on the Netflix sequel of *The Dark Crystal*)

In the centre of the room, filling much of the floor space, is 'It's a Girl' by the Australian-born, UK-based artist Ron Mueck; the son of German toymakers. It's a 16-foot, hyperrealistic sculpture of a newborn baby, based on photos of the artist's daughter. (Mueck also made, and was inside, Ludo the friendly monster in *Labyrinth*, and was also a creature designer on *The Storyteller*. He got his big break when he impressed Charles Saatchi with a sculpture of Pinocchio he made for a group show curated by his mother-in-law, Paula Rego.)

Rego created a painting series that has been given significant credit for the successful second referendum to make abortion legal in Portugal, and a few pieces from that series are here in this room. Women in domestic settings stare out of the canvas with their legs drawn up, or lie contorted across sofas and men's suit jackets. (In her short book *Happening*, Annie Ernaux writes about her backstreet abortion as a teenage girl in France. When the abortion kicks in, she's in her university dormitory. She describes in Alison L. Strayer's translation "a baby doll dangling from my loins at the end of a reddish cord", like a puppet, and that she was "a wild beast." When I miscarried, hunched over on my knees like a tender gizmo transforming into a slick gremlin on the bathroom floor of a shared flat in Munich, it was more like a small, dark doll.)

Accompanying Rego's paintings are oil pastel drawings by Rachel Louise Hodgson of dolls, lying around but seemingly floating off the page, some fleshy like humans with breasts, some standing and crying.

## LUDO

Ludo is my cat, named after Ludo the cowardly monster in *Labyrinth*, built and embodied by Ron Mueck. She has 'scaredy cat' written on her vet file. When she's sitting a certain way, it's like she only has her two front legs, and is like a little goblin standing and watching me. Cats are the goblins we freely let into the house, that knock things off shelves, demand to be fed, that get under your feet, that sleep on your head, that cause mischief. When the flat is very quiet, I like hearing her walk around, or breathing next to me. She chats at us in the bathroom. She is sneaky, snatching things from our plates, and licking dirty dishes. I have my suspicions that she has squirrelled away all of my precious hairbands. Sometimes she moves like an animatronic puppet and I wonder if she's real. Sometimes we think about when I went to collect her as a kitten and basically stole her from her mother as a baby. She now thinks R. is her mother and I'm her sibling. R. joked that when she dies he would quite like to get her stuffed. Maybe we could have her made into a puppet, made into a work of art.

R. and I made a pilgrimage to the Paula Rego museum when we went to Portugal on our honeymoon. The exhibition on at the time was on her engagement with fairytales. There were painterly retellings of Pinocchio (as a vulnerable human boy), of Snow White (as a man in what looks like a sexual liaison with a wicked stepmother type), hundreds of her fairytale illustrations. In one room there was a collection of sickly and puffy puppets on plinths behind glass, a huge spider puppet on the floor. In another there was 'Prince Pig'—a life-size pig-man made of paper mâché wearing human clothes lolling on a chair covered in blue velvet in the corner of the room, made with her granddaughter Carmen Mueck, an artist, whose dad Ron Mueck used her as inspiration for 'It's a Girl'. 'Prince Pig' reminds me of the parents who turn into pigs in *Spirited Away* (2001), which I only saw for the first time recently while in lockdown. How different my life would have been if I grew up watching Studio Ghibli films! And if I'd had the book *Nursery Rhymes* illustrated by Paula Rego back then, where everyone—woman, man and beast—shows their visceral gobliness, rather than the old book of fairytales I had where the humans look like thin ghosts in a trance. There were also paintings of the figure of the 'Pillowman', an oversized doll-like creature that looks like he's composed of overstuffed pairs of tights, which seduces women, and which tells children the misery they will experience in life so they can commit suicide. Rachel Louise Hodgson's stuffed creature reminds me a little of 'Pillowman', like it could be Pillowman's ex-wife who avenges all the women and children.

A few days before leaving for Portugal, we had gone to Tate
Modern to see Jordan Wolfson's installation 'Colored Sculpture'.
'Colored Sculpture' is a seven foot high puppet of a boy held
up and controlled by chains in a kind of rig, endlessly dragged
and smashed into the floor: Pinocchio (or a real boy?) becomes a
punching bag. Puppets often seem creepy because their eyes are
fixed, here the puppet's eyes are screens showing wide, blinking
blue eyes, or sometimes cupcakes bouncing over footage of Betty
Boop and emojis, and which literally follow visitors around the

room. The room echoes with the sound of chains buzzing like a chainsaw, the puppet smashing into the ground, juxtaposed with infrequent bursts of the song 'When a Man Loves a Woman.' The puppet's glossy paint has been scraped grey in places, like worn down horses on a fairground merry-go-round.

I watched videos of one of Wolfson's pieces before seeing it, 'Female Figure', a robot made to look like a nubile young woman wearing a white minidress and thigh-high boots, streaked with dirt, dancing erotically in front of a mirror with pointy teeth like a wolf and wearing a mask over the top half of its face with the glistening green, warty skin of a witch or a goblin. It's protruding, hooked nose is like the masks worn at the masquerade ball in *Labyrinth*. It's impaled through the midriff with a post that attaches it/her to a mirrored wall, and it speaks Wolfson's suggestive statements while its eyes pierce y/ours. It's a sex object of nightmares. Wolfson himself has been tarred with the goblin brush of late. If I could reprogramme 'Female Figure', I would have it recite quotes from the profile of him in *The New Yorker*. It paints him as a narcissist, a user, a trickster creating provocative art devoid of meaning, a troll:

*Detractors, of whom there are many, interpret Wolfson's work as a noxious expression of privilege, casually appropriating pain he seems unlikely to have experienced personally [...] He turns other humans into a prop for his dominance and forced intimacy [...] Sociopaths are people who regard people as objects.*

If either of them is truly subversive, it's obviously Rego. Rego empowers women and children in her work, she lets women fuck pigs and have abortions as if casting a spell, and children murder beasts. Wolfson shows us male fantasies and the male fear of women, and the enactment of violence against a child-like figure, both saying creepy things in his "bedroom voice," as the article puts it. They're objects given the chance to be human and then reobjectified, they are imprisoned and under his spell, like his fans enchanted by his 'subversive' charm. Rachel Louise Hodgson's video where she wears an egg box segment on her nose and spits out a small doll is like a Regoesque subversion of Wolfson's 'Female Figure': a real goblinette, daring to expel a foetus.

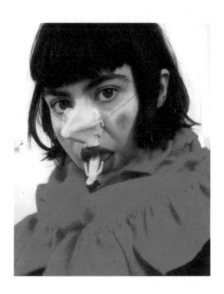

# PART THREE

# GOBLINCORE

## GOBLIN IN A BAND

I thought long and hard about why I had become mesmerised
by awful music men in the past and I had the realisation that
I didn't want to be *with* them, or to *inspire* them, I wanted to *be*
them. Johanna Hedva, in her idolising essay of Nine Inch Nails
guitarist Robin Finck, puts the conflict at the centre of this common
desire/projection relationship much better than I ever could:

*The* fuck vs. be *configuration of rock-star fandom has never made much*
*sense to me. Rock music elementally is about how wanting to fuck someone*
*converges dangerously and deliciously with wanting to be someone. The*
*maxim is meant to explain how much desire has accumulated around the*
*band, not only in terms of how we lust after them, but in terms of something*
*that cuts closer to how we desire ourselves. Audiences, as much as they are*
*fans of particular figures, want to see themselves reflected back through*
*those figures. All good rock stars have a bewitching power that goes straight*

*through the sternum and touches something quivering and central in the gut. It's the feeling that you can find yourself, or who you want to be, in one of the musicians onstage.*

I was on the path of musicianhood when I first started going to gigs at the Atomic, but I got distracted, entranced. I remember the long chats with musicians, especially drummers, asking them about their equipment, about band dynamics, about touring, collecting signed drumsticks, which I would use, mismatched and splintered, to practice beats and rolls on my thighs or on a pillow on my knees, sitting on my bed in my depressing bedsit. But my questions would be waylaid by musicians' advances (*what were we talking about again?*), and I started to believe that consumption—consuming and being consumed—was my only purpose in a music scene. I had given up drum lessons in Munich after my drum teacher told me in his dingy drumming basement that women lacked the strength to play the drums well. I started playing drums and singing in a couple of bands at university, and then eventually joined Sauna Youth as a vocalist, then our alter-ego Monotony on drums. Around the same time, I started the band Feature with a friend, and we went on to be a three-piece, all women.

I cannot tell you how many goblins I've had to deal with along the way. But I'll try. There was the time Sauna Youth played in London and R. shouted from behind the drums 'it's getting tense!' while L. changed a string on his guitar. A man shouted 'I bet she's tense!' nodding in my direction. After we finished playing, a man who was part of the headliner's entourage asked me if I wanted to "go fuck somewhere". When Feature showed up at a pub in Nottingham, all of us carrying guitars and drum gear, some pot-bellied men holding pints standing outside said to us, laughing, "This is a pub, not a knocking shop." (Of course, it's not insulting to be inferred to be a sex worker, but it is to be publicly sexualised while carrying musical equipment and for wearing shorts on a July day). I've had drummers tell me my drumming was 'cute', one even saying "When I saw you were going to play drums, I thought it wouldn't be any good, but you were actually alright." After a show drumming in Monotony, I overheard one man whisper to another, 'Did you see they have a *girl* drummer'. After a show in Hebden Bridge, a man slapped my backside while I was kneeling on stage packing up because I wouldn't talk to him immediately. I remember a man, who was about a foot taller than me, squaring up to me because I told him to tell his friend to stop filming and laughing right in the faces of the all-women band my friends played in. He then tried to stroke/grab my hair when Sauna Youth played later on. Some goblins are even worse because they *try hard to outwardly pretend* not to be goblins. Men I admired and played shows with and who I thought respected me as a peer revealed themselves in the dark. One DMd me once after supporting his band to say he had a dream that I had told him I loved him and had kissed him and that it had been 'embarrassing' for him, making me feel like a goblin even though it was his own (probably fake) dream! I wrote a whole tour diary once when we were going round Europe that comprised solely of goblinating incidents like these. I recently translated the tour diary of Marlene Marder, the guitarist from the Swiss all-women punk band Kleenex, where she sets out many experiences I and others have shared, the harassment, the assault, sexist reviews that were identical to ones I've read in recent years for bands with women in. Nothing much has changed since the 70s.

*It's not fair, but that's the...!*

It really doesn't have to be this way.

## GOBLIN AT THE WRONG TIME,
## FOR THE WRONG REASONS

On the later tours, I started to become unapproachable. I spat on stage. I hated any man coming near me, either before or during a show. I took a man's camera off of him while he filmed us. I told men to stop or blocked them with my body when they were moshing too violently. We played a floor show in Bordeaux or Marseille where a man stood about two foot from my face waggling his tongue at me for most of the show. The next day Sauna Youth played in a bar in Rennes. Right before the gig a photographer wanted to take our picture out the back. 'Let's have the *girl* at the front,' he said, not looking at me. I refused to move, 'No thanks, you're alright'. Eventually I gave up and stood and smiled to get it over with for the others. There was a tiny, low stage. We were crammed onto it with the drumkit and amps. I was standing at the front. The small bar was rammed, a man was standing basically inches from me, just lower down than me. I was pissed off that he was so close to me. It gave me flashbacks of the night before. Looking down at this man I wanted to teach him who the goblin was. For the entirety of one of the songs I hunched down and shout-sang in his face, staring into his eyes. He looked uncomfortable, and I was pleased. Then I heard him quietly say, in an embarrassed way, 'Please, stop. Please.' I stood up straight, and I felt ashamed, and knew I didn't want to be that kind of goblin.

I feel like I'm in a labyrinth and just when I think I've found my way out I fall into a trap.

## GOBLIN TOWN

The band Ravioli Me Away have a song called 'Goblin Town'
and the video charts three bizarre Brit caricatures brandishing
Costa coffee takeaway cups, almond milk, empty beer cans and
a mannequin baby going house-hunting with a greasy letting
agent from Gob Lets who's always on rollerblades. When one
of them signs a house contract with a pen emblazoned with the
Union Jack, she starts transforming into a goblin.

## GOBLINCORE

I met my friend Luke for a coffee and knew he would be the right
person to ask about goblins in musical terms. If you had to describe
a musician as a goblin, who would you choose, and is there such
a thing as goblincore, other than the twee online movement where
people share photos of idyllic cottages, perfect picnics, fairytale-
inspired fashion, as well as a lot of frog and possum memes and
very few goblins? I gave him a few suggestions to start him off:
Lars Ulrich, Morrissey, Glenn "Hack the heads off little girls
and put them on my wall" Danzig of course. Luke's face lit up:
Yes, Lars is the prototypical goblin, Danzig is more like a cave
troll, Thom Yorke, John Lydon (disgusting creature, his recent
appearance on stage in a cloak was pretty goblinesque), Morrissey
has a mischievous bent and, no goblincore, but... had I heard of
*dungeon synth*, and surely Mortiis? Our friend Marcus was on the
way: "Hold the dungeon door open for me!" Marcus said that a
goblin should be small and wiry, no more than 5'8", perhaps with
a pot belly, he would consider Danzig, for instance, to be more
an Urak-hai, those creatures bred in Isengard in *Lord of the Rings*.
Don't forget the band Goblin—Italosynth—and Goblin Cock,
stoner metal. If a goblin wore a T-shirt it would be a tight ringer
tee, they decided.

If goblincore existed and could be summed up in a single figurehead, there are many contenders for me. Ellie May Roberts from Good Throb wearing shredded bin liners and jiffy cloths, marigold gloves, her front teeth blackened; Alli Logout of Special Interest in a variety of leather and mesh combos. (There was going to be one more, but it turned out he was a goblin.) The two I would ultimately pick are: Mary-Jane Dunphe of Vexx and Emil Bognar-Nasdor of Dawn of Humans.

When Dawn of Humans play, the lighting has to be just right. Very dark, pitch black. Strobes. Emil is often naked, covered in streaks of black body paint, sometimes with shards of mirror covering his penis; like a *golem* covered in mud. There's a video of him popping up and down in a mirrored cube in The Print Shop at MOMA PS1 in New York like a jack-in-the-box, naked except for a swathe of tin foil from the box packaging with some as a crown for his head, both soon lost to the throng. Emil is compact and muscular, yet commanding, and his voice is like metal grinding against slate.

Like Emil, Mary-Jane is a performance artist who has irresistible charisma and presence, and I've been transfixed by her every time I've seen her perform. She contorts herself, wild-eyed, her face screwed up, each show is a largely improvised movement piece, stretch and twist, so artful and so unpredictable. Lie down, kneel, up on tiptoes and fall from a height. What I love about watching MJ perform is that, be it a matinee or midnight show, she's always full goblin. Watching her form a corridor through a rammed crowd simply by walking straight through it, refusing to move or stop, looking people in the eye all the while, when people expect her to stay put, be watched, behave herself, made me smile wickedly.

I emailed MJ to see what she thought about being referred to as a goblin? I explained that in my head I would often think about performances as percentages—my bandmates would often joke before a show whether I was going to give it 8% or 20% or 60% etc—but that I also thought about how goblin I was going to be, a bit goblin, quite goblin, I don't think I'd ever reached full goblin. She replied...

*I am honored to be a goblin in your eyes. It's funny you write out goblin percentages because since I first started playing shows and doing weird performance, I would figure out if I could go half goblin or full goblin that night. Or sometimes I would go half goblin on just a normal day for some reason. It's that little imp of the perverse, sometimes it's good at dancing.*

She also plays in the band Pinocchio, where she paints her face to look like a marionette.

### FULL GOBLIN

Up until a year or two ago I wanted to be quite anti-performance— I didn't want to be a performing woman, an entertaining puppet. I realised over time that showing I was having fun, showing that I was the one in control, was a far more powerful thing. Now I laugh and smile with my eyes wide open, I screw up my face and snarl. I remembered why I liked being at punk shows, the moshing, the camaraderie, the freedom to be other.

Sauna Youth were invited to play a festival in Munich the day before my thirty-second birthday, and I decided that if I was ever going to go full goblin, it would be there, in the city where I promised myself I would one day be in a band, where I was made to feel like I wasn't the right kind of goblin.

In a big theatre on the street parallel to the Neuturmstrasse and the former Atomic Café the four of us warmed up in the dressing room by jumping up and down on the spot to burn off excess energy like Fireys losing their heads, and then we played twenty odd songs back to back for an hour in a huge, packed theatre emptied of its seats and with people up to the ceiling on balconies. I fantasised that I was the lead in a goblin opera, my voice reverberated deafeningly loud, my shadow was thrown massive onto the back wall like a shadow puppet in the telling of a fairytale, I was Medusa staring down the whole room with a smile on my lips, and I forgot who I was while being all me.

# GOODBYE
# GOBLINS

I only realised this year that *Labyrinth*'s true plot arc is that Sarah is reliving her late mother's role as an actress in the play 'Labyrinth' to find closure for her death. Dorothy's second adventure in Oz is a kind of immersive form of therapy. Like Sarah and Dorothy, submerging myself in these fantasy worlds (both filmic and private), for perhaps the final time for a while, has been soothing, but has shown me how much I need to move on.

After all, I'm the storyteller now.

*Goodbye Dorothy! Goodbye Sarah!*
*Should you need us... for any reason at all. Yes, should you need us...*

*I need you, I don't know why but...every now and then in my life...for no reason at all... I need you.*